THE UNOFFICIAL GUIDE T

SONG CONTEST
UNITED KINGDOM
LIVERPOOL 2023

After a hiatus of 25 years, the Eurovision Song Contest, the world's largest live music event, returns to the United Kingdom and will take place in Liverpool in May 2023. Ukraine, the previous year's winner, will co-host the event with Liverpool serving as the host city. The contest will span three live shows, with two semi-finals scheduled for Tuesday, May 9th and Thursday, May 11th, respectively, and the Grand Final on Saturday, May 13th. The M&S Bank Arena will serve as the venue for the event, while the Eurovision Village and EuroClub will also be located in Liverpool.

As a UNESCO Music City with a rich musical legacy, Liverpool is proud to have birthed countless music legends, including The Beatles, Cilla Black, Dead or Alive, Frankie Goes to Hollywood, Melanie C, Atomic Kitten, Sugababes, and Sonia, who was the runner-up in 1993. The city boasts a remarkable record of almost 60 UK Singles Chart No.1s.

Liverpool is also home to the Royal Liverpool Philharmonic Orchestra, one of Europe's finest orchestras, which resides in the stunning art deco building of the Philharmonic Hall located on Hope Street.

The United Kingdom did not win the Eurovision Song Contest, but it was chosen to host the event after the winning country declined the automatic hosting right or was unable to host for various reasons. The European Broadcasting Union (EBU) has the right to offer the opportunity to another broadcaster, with the most likely candidate being a country that finished in the top five places, especially if it is one of the "Big Five" financial contributors to the EBU.

Ukraine expressed interest in hosting, but the ongoing Russian invasion and subsequent war made it an impractical option for EBU organizers. As a result, the United Kingdom's BBC was offered the hosting rights and accepted them.

How did Liverpool become the chosen host city for Eurovision 2023? Initially, seven cities, including

Newcastle, Manchester, Leeds, Glasgow, Liverpool, Sheffield, and Birmingham, were shortlisted as potential hosts. A two-way run-off between Glasgow and Liverpool took place, with Liverpool emerging victorious. ESC Executive Supervisor Martin Österdahl cited Liverpool's association with music and the suitability of Liverpool Arena as a venue for a global event of this magnitude. He also commended the city's inclusive ideas for showcasing last year's winners, Ukraine, to the thousands of fans expected to visit Liverpool in May.

Travel

Liverpool is the sixth-largest metropolitan area in the UK, and has a rich history as an important port city that was bolstered by the Industrial Revolution. The city also has a significant music and sport heritage. Liverpool is easily accessible by air, road, rail, and sea, making it a convenient destination for Eurovision 2023. Liverpool John Lennon Airport is the city's primary airport and deals exclusively in European destinations. It is located about 12 km from the city centre, and the best way to get to the city is by bus or taxi. Manchester Airport, located around 50 km from Liverpool, is another major airport that serves both European and longer-haul routes. Two other airports to consider are Leeds Bradford Airport and Birmingham Airport. Dublin, Belfast, and Douglas (Isle of Man) are connected to Liverpool by sea.

Liverpool has a well-connected transport system,

with Merseyrail operating the train network across Merseyside. The city centre has four main train stations, namely Liverpool Lime Street, Liverpool Central, Moorfields, and James Street.

If you prefer to travel by bus, Arriva offers an extensive bus network across the wider Liverpool area, with Liverpool One serving as the primary hub in the city centre. To make your bus journeys more affordable, there's a convenient three-day adult ticket available for £12.50, which equates to £4.17 per day if you plan on using the bus several times a day. This option is slightly cheaper than the day pass (£4.60). For even better value, you may opt for the weekly ticket (£17.00), which costs only £2.43 per day.

The M&S Bank Arena

The M&S Bank Arena, formerly known as the Echo Arena, will be the venue for Eurovision 2023 in Liverpool. Despite having a capacity of only 11,000, which is half the size of arenas in London and Manchester, Liverpool's walkability was a significant factor in winning the bid. Tickets for the nine shows will be released on Ticketmaster.co.uk on Tuesday 7th March. Eurovision Village will be located at the Pier Head and will host street artists, fashion designers, and a culture trail featuring local Eurovision legend, Sonia. EuroClub will be held at Camp & Furnace, a versatile industrial venue in Liverpool's Baltic Triangle, and will feature nightly club events, post-show after-parties, and special events celebrating competing nations. Bingo Lingo will host two special events at Camp & Furnace on Friday 5th May and Saturday 6th May, with tickets available on Skiddle.

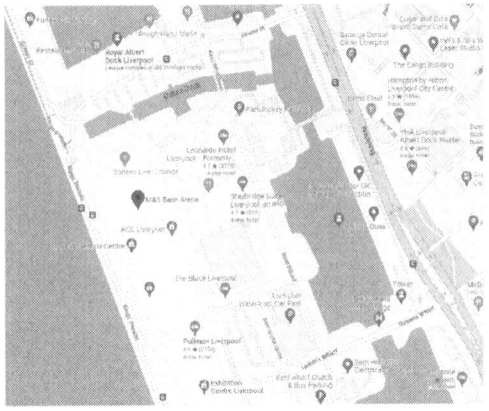

The M&S Arena Seating Plan

THE UNOFFICIAL GUIDE TO THE LIVERPOOL EUROVISION S...

Eurofest

EuroFest, a cultural festival, is set to take place in Liverpool for two weeks leading up to the Eurovision Song Contest Grand Final. From May 1 to May 14, 24 new commissions, 19 of which are collaborations between United Kingdom and Ukrainian artists, will transform the city as fans from all over the world come to Liverpool. While complete details of all the projects will be released later in March, four headline plans have been revealed. The festival will be inspired by the Eurovision 2023 slogan "United By Music". The Kazimier will present The Blue and Yellow Submarine Parade, a massive outdoor underwater sea disco that will kick off the Eurovision Party. The English National Opera will create a unique show called The English National Opera does Eurovision, which will combine two distinct musical worlds into one epic outdoor performance with live chorus and orchestra. Ukrainian artist Katya Buchatska's Izyum to Liverpool will transform Liverpool Cathedral into a train carriage that replicates the journey from Izyum to the Polish border. Finally, Rave Ukraine, a collaboration between Jez Collins, UAME I Music Saves UA, and Open Culture, will simultaneously hold a rave in Liverpool and Kyiv, which will be streamed globally. The festival will have mass participation events, and more information on how to participate will be provided in the coming weeks. Several organizations will participate in EuroFest, including the BBC Storyville Live, English National Opera, Tate Liverpool, and others. The artists were chosen through a process that included the BBC, British Council, Ukrainian Institute, and Culture Liverpool, and the festival will feature collaborations between artists from the UK and Ukraine.

Concert Square

Concert Square, in the city center, will host a variety of events and performances, including tribute acts, live performers, drag shows, and screenings of both Semi-Finals. Meanwhile, six consecutive nights of "Eurovision madness" will take place at Fusion Liverpool, with fan-organized EUROfansClub and the annual WiwiJam, organized by fan site WiwiBloggs.

The event will be headlined by The Roop, Rasmussen, Anxhela Peristeri, Kate Ryan, and Destiny from Malta, among others. Mersey Ferries will also offer on-board events throughout Eurovision week.

Ten Things to See Whilst in Liverpool

1. THE BEATLES MUSEUM

One of the must-see attractions in Liverpool is the Liverpool Beatles Museum, which is located just a stone's throw away from the iconic Cavern Club. As the birthplace of the Beatles, the museum houses an extensive collection of authentic artifacts and instruments used by the band, as well as over 1,000 pieces of Beatles memorabilia. The museum's three floors offer an immersive audio-visual experience that will delight any Beatles fan. Visitors can marvel at John Lennon's Sergeant Pepper medals, Paul McCartney's bass amp, George Harrison's guitar, Ringo's Ludwig snare drum and stool, and even Pete Best's Premier drum kit from 1960-1962. Additionally, the museum features never-before-seen letters, exclusive interviews with the band members, and previously unseen footage of the Beatles. If you're in Liverpool for Eurovision 2023, a visit to the Liverpool Beatles Museum is an absolute must.

It's worth noting that there are actually two Beatles Museums in Liverpool! Both places are worth visiting, but they are quite different. The Beatles Story (as the name suggests) takes the visitor through the story of the Beatles using mocked-up scenes and displays. The Magical Beatles Museum houses many, many authentic items, including letters, bits of film, and clothing.

How to Get There

This museum is located at 23 Mathew Street in Liverpool, which is actually just a stone's throw away from the Cavern Club, one of the most famous sites in Beatles history.

The closest bus stops are near the corner of Cook Street and North John Street. There is also a stop on Lord Street a few blocks south. You'll find the closest underground station at Moorfields to the north, but the James Street station is also just a few blocks away.

Many Liverpool Beatles tours will pass by this location due to its proximity to the Cavern Club, so this could be another great way to find the museum without too much trouble.

2.
The Beatles Story Museum

The Beatles Story is a must-visit attraction in Liverpool, especially for those with a passion for all things Beatles. This immersive museum takes you on a journey through the history of the Fab Four, with exhibits and attractions that bring to life the excitement and energy of Beatlemania in the 1960s. From a replica of the iconic Cavern Club to Abbey Road Studios and a Yellow Submarine, The Beatles Story is filled with interactive displays, memorabilia, and photographs that showcase the band's incredible musical legacy. With the 'Living History' audio guide, you can delve even deeper into the Beatles' story and learn about their personal lives and behind-the-scenes moments that helped shape their music.

3. The Magical Mystery Tour and the cavern

Experience the glory days of Beatlemania with the Magical Mystery Tour around Liverpool. Even if you don't get to do Carpool Karaoke with Sir Paul McCartney, the Magical Mystery Tour bus is the next best thing! Immerse yourself in Liverpool's rich pop music heritage as classic Beatles tuncs play in the background and a knowledgeable tour guide provides insightful commentary. Visit the homes of John, Paul, George, and Ringo, along with other key locations where The Beatles legend was written. After the tour, head over to the world-famous Cavern Club to sip a drink and Twist and Shout to live music from the Cavern's resident musicians. This iconic club is where the Beatles honed their craft and skyrocketed to British stardom. Visit each of the band members' childhood homes and the places that inspired their hits, such as Strawberry Fields and Penny Lane.

4. The British Music Experience

This fantastic interactive attraction is perfect for both musicians and pop music enthusiasts alike.Travel through the decades and explore the history of British pop and rock music, from the heights of Beatlemania to the New Wave synth-pop and hair metal of the 80s, to the Britpop of the 90s and the indie revival of the mid-2000s. Marvel at costumes, instruments, and memorabilia from iconic artists like The Beatles, David Bowie, Adele, and Oasis as you wander through eight themed zones bursting with musical greatness.

But the real thrill comes from the Gibson Interactive Studio, where musicians of all levels can let loose and rock out on legendary instruments like Les Paul guitars, Roland synthesizers, and professional vocal booths. Who knows? Your own musical genius might just earn you a place in the museum someday!

5. Strawberry Fields

Strawberry Fields, a cultural hidden gem in Liverpool, is a must-visit destination for Beatles enthusiasts. Despite not being a music-themed attraction, it is steeped in formative Beatles history. John Lennon, the legendary pop icon, songwriter, and peace advocate, spent his childhood playing in the garden of the nearby Strawberry Field children's home run by the

Salvation Army. His love for the place inspired him to write the famous song "Strawberry Fields Forever". This self-guided tour offers visitors a chance to explore this little corner of cultural history and learn about the place that inspired one of the brightest young artists of the 20th century, as well as countless more disadvantaged kids who lived and played here.

Using a multimedia guide, visitors can explore archival footage and photographs that document the history of the facility and its most famous young visitor. Strawberry Field also houses the 'Imagine More' Café, where you can enjoy locally sourced breakfast, afternoon tea, Sunday lunch, hot drinks, and more in warm and welcoming indoor and outdoor seating areas. After the loud and proud glitz and glamour of Eurovision 2023, Strawberry Fields is the perfect soulful place to chill and recuperate.

6. Liverpool FC Stadium Guided tour

A visit to Liverpool for Eurovision 2023 would be incomplete without a stop at the UK's most successful football club in European competitions. Anfield has hosted countless legendary European football matches and is consistently ranked as one of the best stadiums in the world for its electric atmosphere. Even without match tickets, you can still experience the best of Anfield.

Indulge in the Liverpool FC Stadium Tour + Audio Guide, where the lively match-day ambiance is matched only by the personality and unrelenting Scouse accents of the tour guides! With this guided audio tour, you'll have the chance to explore the dressing rooms, participate in a press conference, and uncover the secrets of Liverpool FC's illustrious past. Moreover, a state-of-the-art multimedia handset will provide you with exclusive footage, interviews, and other extra content.

Lastly, make your way to the museum for a captivating exhibit showcasing the Reds' history, complete with numerous trophies, as well as an array of interactive displays highlighting the club's remarkable legacy.

Built in 1884, Anfield was initially rented by Everton FC. The first game at the stadium was played on September 28, 1884, with Everton securing a 5-0 victory over Earlstown.

However, in 1891, a rent dispute with the landlord forced Everton to vacate Anfield, and the newly-formed Liverpool FC took up residence a year later. Their first game at the stadium was a resounding 7-1 win over Rotherham.

In the late 19th and early 20th century, Anfield underwent various renovations, including the construction of a new main stand designed by Archibald Leitch in 1895 and the famous Spion Kop ten years later.

For the following two decades, Anfield remained largely unchanged until the expansion of the Kop in 1928, increasing its capacity to around 30,000 spectators.

Anfield's record attendance of 61,905 was set

in 1958 during a match between Liverpool and Wolverhampton Wanderers. Between 1963 and 1973, the old Main Stand was demolished and replaced with a new one, further improving the stadium.

7. The Dark Side of Liverpool Ghost History Tour

Embark on a spine-tingling 1.5-hour historical ghost tour of Liverpool's colorful cultural quarter and discover its most famous ghosts and grisly stories. This unique tour takes you down Hope Street, Liverpool's most haunted street, where you'll start outside the city's most famous ale house and visit two awe-inspiring cathedrals.

Along the way, you'll see the famous Everyman

Theatre, the Rodney Street Conservation Area, and the building where John Lennon lived for three years. Your guides will also reveal the spot where Hitler's brother hid to avoid conscription.

The tour culminates in St James' Gardens, the final resting place of 58,000 souls, and the awe-inspiring Gothic Anglican Cathedral cemetery. Here, you'll hear tales of the black plague and Liverpool's most famous ghost story. With an expert guide and an open mind, prepare to experience the dark side of Liverpool on this eerie journey.

8. City Explorer: Hop On, Hop Off Liverpool Sightseeing Bus Tour

Bringing the very best of Liverpool to you at an unbeatable price. This hop on hop off sightseeing tour has been carefully designed to give you the freedom to explore many of Liverpool's top attractions. There's an informative guide onboard each tour to help you explore and talk you through the history, drama, talent and humour that's made Liverpool what it is today. Hop on and off as often as you like. Whether a long lunch beckons or some serious retail therapy calls, just hop on the bus and explore more of the sights.

9. ST JOHNS BEACON Viewing Gallery Experience

Radio City, one of the UK's most successful radio stations, gives you a unique opportunity to view Merseyside's ever changing skyline over 400 feet above the heart of the city centre. St Johns Beacon, one of Liverpool's most iconic landmarks, offers breath taking panoramic views of the Wirral, North Wales, Lancashire and as far as Snowdonia and Blackpool on clearer days.

10. Liverpool Cathedral

Why visit? At the centre of the city lies a Gothic giant that will leave you awestruck. Liverpool Cathedral, the largest religious building in Britain and the fifth-largest cathedral in the world, was constructed from 1904 to 1978 and is now accessible to visitors every day of the year. Feast your eyes on the world's highest and widest Gothic arches, the UK's largest organ, and a stunning display of stained-glass windows. The cathedral also hosts year-round art exhibitions and charitable events, so be sure to consult the website before you go.

Events
Sam Ryder Spaceman Eurovision outfit to go ON display at the BME in Liverpool

Sam Ryder's outfit, which he wore on stage during the Eurovision Song Contest 2022, will be displayed to the public at the British Music Experience (BME) in Liverpool on 22 March 2023. The exhibit will be showcased before the city hosts the upcoming song contest. Sam Ryder is a popular British singer-songwriter who rose to fame on TikTok during the Covid-19 lockdowns. He represented the UK in the Eurovision Song Contest 2022 in Turin, Italy, with his song "Space Man," which won first place in the jury vote and second overall. His black denim jumpsuit was adorned with jeweled glass crystals, beads, pearls, and embroidered symbols of the sun, moon, planets, and stars, reminiscent of the stage outfits of legendary performers such as Ziggy Stardust, Queen, and Elton John.

Sam Ryder's jumpsuit was designed by stylist Luke Day, who drew inspiration from iconic performers such as Bowie and Elvis, as well as Sam's passion for astronomy and astrology. The design also includes a subtle nod to the Union Jack. The suit took over 210 hours to create and was embroidered with over 15,000 beads and gems. Sam Ryder considers the jumpsuit a turning point in his personal journey with music and a significant moment in the UK's performance in the Eurovision Song Contest 2022.

The BME is delighted to display Sam Ryder's jumpsuit, which they describe as one of the great stage outfits of the present day. Executive Director Liz Koravos highlights the meaningful stories that the outfit represents, from Sam's successes to Eurovision's ethos of inclusion and unity. Head of UNESCO City of Music for Liverpool, Kevin McManus, believes that the display of the outfit is a real coup for the BME and will be a treat for Eurovision fans visiting the city. The British Music Experience charts the history of rock and pop music from 1945 to the present day, featuring instruments and stage outfits worn by some of the UK's most popular artists. The archive includes Eurovision successes such as Lulu, Sandie Shaw, and Bucks Fizz, as well as heritage greats like David Bowie, Queen, and Elton John. Visitors can also support the Museum by Gift Aiding the cost of admission. Additionally, the BME will be hosting a special event with Sam Ryder on Saturday 25 March 2023, ahead of his performance at The O2 Academy, Liverpool. More information can be found on the British Music Experience website and social media feeds.

THE UNOFFICIAL GUIDE TO THE LIVERPOOL EUROVISION S...

Eurovision 2023: The Blue and Yellow Submarine Parade

The Blue and Yellow Submarine Parade through Liverpool is definitely going to be one of the most spectacular large-scale events happening in the run up to Eurovision.

And, not only are huge crowds expected to turn out to see the underwater-themed disco partying its way through the streets on Friday May 5, but people can get involved in it too. The parade, which will be a highlight of the pre-contest cultural celebrations, will feature a giant drumming octopus, jellyfish and a big disco puffer fish as well as the iconic submarine. There are a few different zones along the route of the parade such as the octopus garden, jellyfish junction, and crustacean station," adds Laura. "All these different places have a little theme around them and we're going to encourage the public to pick an area and then dress in line with that theme. The idea is that all the public who come and watch the parade will essentially be a part of it because they'll be dressed in line with one of the big floats and one of the areas.

St Georges Hall to host Eurovision Extravaganza series of events during the week of the competition

The St George's Hall Eurovision Extravaganza will be held from Wednesday 10th to Saturday 13th May, featuring a series of events. On the first day, there will be guided tours showcasing Liverpool's musical history and journey to becoming the host city of Eurovision 2023. Additionally, the St George's Hall Charitable Trust will partner with organist Lee Ward to present the best of Eurovision on the 7,737 piped Willis Organ, with all proceeds going to the Trust.

The second semi-final of the Eurovision Song Contest 2023 will be screened live on Thursday 11th May, supported by entertainment acts and presented in partnership with LCR Pride Foundation and ASG Audio Visual. The event will be hosted by Brenda LeBeau, a drag queen and cabaret artist, and will feature after-show DJs, Sonic Yootha.

On Friday 12th May, an ABBA tribute night will be held in honor of the 1974 Eurovision Song Contest winners, providing live music entertainment. The program will culminate on Saturday 13th May with the Eurovision Song Contest 2023 Grand Final, featuring acts supported by LCR Pride Foundation and ASG Audio Visual.

During the events, the Homebaked Bakery team will be selling their Peace Pie, and £1 from each pie sold will be donated to DEC Humanitarian Appeal in Ukraine and Fans Supporting Foodbanks.

Additionally, Liverpool Town Hall will host a concert performance of Eurovision classics by the Didsbury String Quartet on Thursday 11th May. The event promises to offer a sensory feast for attendees, with a limited number of ticket upgrades available that include a guided tour of the Town Hall prior to the event.

Hannah Sweeney, Head of Venue Operations at Liverpool City Halls, expressed excitement about the Eurovision events, noting the key role played by St George's Hall in hosting the live Semi Final Draw and the National Lottery's Big Eurovision Welcome. Andi Herring, CEO of LCR Pride Foundation, emphasized the event's partnership and collaboration, with the goal of celebrating the contest, Liverpool's LGBT+ community, and the Ukrainian community. Cabinet Member for Culture & Visitor Economy, Cllr Harry Doyle, encouraged everyone to participate in the events, as they offer something for everyone, regardless of their interests.

The British Eurovision Song: Mae Muller has been chosen as the UK's representative for the Eurovision Song Contes

Mae Muller has been chosen as the UK's representative for the Eurovision Song Contest which will be held in Liverpool in May. The 25-year-old singer-songwriter will perform her track 'I Wrote A Song', which was selected following a search by the BBC and TaP Music. The announcement was made on the BBC Radio 2 Breakfast Show by Zoe Ball and Rylan Clark on March 9. Muller gained mainstream attention after releasing her single 'Better Days' in collaboration with NEIKED and Polo G, which charted in the top 40 in both the UK and the US. The last time the UK won the contest was in 1997 with 'Love Shine A Light'. Muller was born the same year, but hopes to replicate the success with her performance this year.

Muller began writing music at the age of 8 and pursued her dream career in music after leaving her job at American Apparel to work in a pub in Kentish

Town. She uploaded her songs to Soundcloud and Instagram in 2017, which led to her discovery and signing by Capitol. She has released several EPs and her debut studio album 'Chapter 1' in 2019. Muller's promotional strategy ahead of the contest will be crafted by TaP Music, which has also helped revamp the UK's Eurovision strategy after years of disappointing results.

Printed in Great Britain
by Amazon